Created by Anna and Debbie Yarwood

https://thesmartermanager.com

INTRODUCTION

As a manager, we can get caught up in busyness. We have a team to lead, deadlines to meet, a boss to keep happy and far too many meetings to attend.

So much to do and never enough time. It can feel like a hamster wheel, with one day crashing into the next before we can catch a breath.

Sometimes we have to slow down to speed up. I see you raising your eyebrows but hear me out. We can get caught up in the 'doing' as a manager. And we don't spend enough time thinking about whether we are doing the right things.

WHEN TIME MANAGEMENT TOOLS DON'T WORK

In the past, I've searched for time management techniques hoping (often desperately) that they would help me feel less overwhelmed and get on top of a never ending to-do list.

I was often left frustrated though. It felt like no-one had a job like mine. I never knew what would come up each day. I was constantly fighting fires. And customers were loud and often angry - all wanting to be top of the list.

What I did learn - eventually - is that I needed to take some control. I had become a slave to the most urgent items on my to do list. I was overwhelmed and exhausted. I needed to carve out some time to not only think about how to move forward but also to make sure I was being the leader my team needed me to be.

> ## 'Plans are nothing. Planning is everything'
> ### - Dwight W Eisenhower

You may want to tell me that you have no time to plan. Or that there is no point as everything changes in a heartbeat anyway.

I get it. Because I have said the very same things. And I guarantee that there will be many times that some fire breaks out and your well thought out plan feels completely pointless.

When that happens a few weeks in a row, you can be forgiven for thinking that there is no point in making a plan in the first place.

But it's not about the plan itself, the value is in the planning process.

Understanding what you have on your plate can help in the following ways:

- Reducing overwhelm (you have more control when you know what you're facing)
- You can delegate work early enough so it can get done in time
- When some unexpected issue arises, you quickly know what may have to be compromised
- You make choices on how to use your time with a clear view of your priorities

Maybe the fire is not be more important than what you already have planned to do. It's easy to check on that with a plan in place If the fire does take priority, you you can communicate early with those impacted by your change of focus.

THE BUSY MANAGER'S PLANNER

The power of this planner is that it encourages you to think ahead and be clear about your priorities and also to reflect on how things are going. If you don't take time to reflect, you can easily fall down the same holes every single day! When you reflect on your behaviours, you can start to learn how to do things differently. This can have a major impact on not only your productivity but also your leadership skills in general.

I'm inviting you to make a choice. You can choose to carry on exactly as you are, or you could choose to find 10 minutes a day to take some control.

Here's how this planner will help

PLANNING
12 Week Goals: Choose up to 4 goals you want to focus on over the next 3 months. They don't have to all be work related #worklifebalance

Weekly Planner: Plan out your week, including how you can progress your 12 week goals

Daily Planner: Take your goals for the week and break them down over your five working days. You'll also be prompted by a daily question to challenge your thinking a little

REVIEW
Weekly Review: At the end of each week, look back on how well it went and what you might do differently next week

Monthly Review: Check in with how well you have led your team this month and what you need to work on in the month to come. You'll find some management tips at the end of the book that may help

HOW IT WORKS

Step 1: Decide on your 12 week goals

Step 2: Plan your week How will you progress your 12 week goals?

Step 3: Break down your weekly goals into daily activity

Step 4: Review your week. What might you do differently next week?

Step 5: Rate your leadership skills in the monthly review

Step 6: What actions will you focus on next month to improve your scores?

And check out the Management Tips at the end of the book to sharpen up your skills

12 WEEK GOALS

From / / To / /

Goal 1:

_____
_____
_____
_____

Goal 2:

_____
_____
_____
_____

Goal 3:

_____
_____
_____
_____

Goal 4:

_____
_____
_____
_____

Great opportunities to help others seldom come, but small ones surround us everyday – Sally Koch

WEEKLY PLANNER

DATE: / /

My Big 3 For This Week

1
2
3

What Obstacles May Get In My Way And How I'll Overcome Them

Other Things To Do This Week

The Advice I Would Give Myself This Week Is

I know how it looks. But just start. Nothing is insurmountable
— Lin-Manuel Miranda

DAILY PLAN

M   T   W   T   F

DATE: /   /

My Big 3 For Today

1 _____

2 _____

3 _____

Other Tasks

- ◼
- ◼
- ◼
- ◼
- ◼
- ◼
- ◼
- ◼
- ◼
- ◼

Which of your strengths will be most useful to use today?

Note To Self:

Be strong, be fearless, be beautiful. And believe that anything is possible when you have the right people there to support you – Misty Copeland

DAILY PLAN

M   T   W   T   F

DATE: /   /

My Big 3 For Today

1

2

3

Other Tasks

- ◼
- ◼
- ◼
- ◼
- ◼
- ◼
- ◼
- ◼
- ◼
- ◼

What will you be more curious about today?

Note To Self:

You cannot discover new oceans unless you have the courage to lose sight of the shore – Andre Gide

DAILY PLAN

M   T   W   T   F   DATE: /   /

My Big 3 For Today

1 _____
2 _____
3 _____

Other Tasks

- _____
- _____
- _____
- _____
- _____
- _____
- _____
- _____
- _____
- _____

When will you need to keep a check on your emotions today?

Note To Self:

When you get tired, learn to rest, not quit
— Banksy

DAILY PLAN

M   T   W   T   F   DATE: /   /

My Big 3 For Today

1 _____

2 _____

3 _____

Other Tasks

- _____
- _____
- _____
- _____
- _____
- _____
- _____
- _____
- _____
- _____

What risk will you take today?

Note To Self:

Doing what you're afraid of, getting out of your comfort zone, taking risks — that's what life is — Amy Poehler

DAILY PLAN

M   T   W   T   F

DATE: / /

My Big 3 For Today

1

2

3

Other Tasks

-
-
-
-
-
-
-
-
-

What will give you energy today?

Note To Self:

Treat the people the way you want to be treated. Talk to people the way you want to be talked to. Respect is earned not given — Anon

WEEKLY REVIEW

DATE: / /

My Biggest Wins

1
2
3
4
5

How Did I Get On With My Weekly Big 3?

1
2
3

Lessons Learnt This Week

1
2
3
4
5

What Would I Do Differently If I Could Start This Week Again?

Own your magic, walk in your purpose, and rock your truth
— Beverly Bond

WEEKLY PLANNER

DATE: / /

My Big 3 For This Week

1 _____

2 _____

3 _____

What Obstacles May Get In My Way And How I'll Overcome Them

_____

_____

_____

_____

_____

Other Things To Do This Week

_____   _____

_____   _____

_____   _____

_____   _____

_____   _____

_____   _____

The Advice I Would Give Myself This Week Is

_____

If you have a goal that is very, very far out, and you approach it in little steps, you start to get there faster – Mae Jemison

DAILY PLAN

M   T   W   T   F

DATE: /   /

My Big 3 For Today

1 _____
2 _____
3 _____

Other Tasks

- _____
- _____
- _____
- _____
- _____
- _____
- _____
- _____
- _____
- _____

What might you procrastinate on today?

Note To Self:

The only way to get a thing done is to start to do it, then keep on doing it, and finally you'll finish it – Langston Hughes

DAILY PLAN

M   T   W   T   F   DATE: /   /

My Big 3 For Today

1

2

3

Other Tasks

- ▪
- ▪
- ▪
- ▪
- ▪
- ▪
- ▪
- ▪
- ▪
- ▪

Where can you have the biggest impact today?

Note To Self:

If you want to do a few things right, do them yourself. If you want to do great things and make a big impact, learn to delegate – John C. Maxwell

DAILY PLAN

M   T   W   T   F

DATE: /   /

My Big 3 For Today

1
2
3

Other Tasks

-
-
-
-
-
-
-
-
-
-

What are you most looking forward to today?

Note To Self:

My mission in life is not merely to survive, but to thrive, and to do so with passion, compassion, humour and style – Maya Angelou

DAILY PLAN

M T W T F   DATE: /   /

My Big 3 For Today

1 _____

2 _____

3 _____

Other Tasks

- ■ _____
- ■ _____
- ■ _____
- ■ _____
- ■ _____
- ■ _____
- ■ _____
- ■ _____
- ■ _____
- ■ _____

What would you like someone to say about you today?

Note To Self:

A good leader is a person who takes a little more than his share of the blame and a little less than his share of the credit – John Maxwell

DAILY PLAN

M T W T F

DATE: / /

My Big 3 For Today

1 _____

2 _____

3 _____

Other Tasks

- _____
- _____
- _____
- _____
- _____
- _____
- _____
- _____
- _____
- _____

What are you most grateful for today?

Note To Self:

Optimism is a happiness magnet. If you stay positive, good things and good people will be drawn to you – Mary Lou Retton

WEEKLY REVIEW

DATE: /   /

My Biggest Wins

1
2
3
4
5

How Did I Get On With My Weekly Big 3?

1
2
3

Lessons Learnt This Week

1
2
3
4
5

What Would I Do Differently If I Could Start This Week Again?

Leadership and learning are indispensable to each other
— John F. Kennedy

WEEKLY PLANNER

DATE: / /

My Big 3 For This Week

1 _____

2 _____

3 _____

What Obstacles May Get In My Way And How I'll Overcome Them

_____
_____
_____
_____
_____

Other Things To Do This Week

_____   _____
_____   _____
_____   _____
_____   _____
_____   _____
_____   _____

The Advice I Would Give Myself This Week Is

_____

This is your Monday morning reminder that you can handle whatever this week throws at you – Unknown

DAILY PLAN

M   T   W   T   F

DATE: /   /

My Big 3 For Today

1 _____

2 _____

3 _____

Other Tasks

- _____
- _____
- _____
- _____
- _____
- _____
- _____
- _____
- _____
- _____

What should you say yes to today?

Note To Self:

If you want something you've never had, you must be willing to do something you've never done - Thomas Jefferson

DAILY PLAN

M T W T F

DATE: / /

My Big 3 For Today

1

2

3

Other Tasks

-
-
-
-
-
-
-
-
-
-

How will you make today special?

Note To Self:

I have discovered in life that there are ways of getting almost anywhere you want to go, if you really want to go — Langston Hughes

DAILY PLAN

M   T   W   T   F   DATE: / /

My Big 3 For Today

1 _____

2 _____

3 _____

Other Tasks

- ☐ _____
- ☐ _____
- ☐ _____
- ☐ _____
- ☐ _____
- ☐ _____
- ☐ _____
- ☐ _____
- ☐ _____
- ☐ _____

What could get in the way of today being a success?

Note To Self:

Take chances. Mistakes are never a failure – they can be turned into wisdom – Cat Cora

DAILY PLAN

M   T   W   T   F

DATE: /   /

My Big 3 For Today

1 _____

2 _____

3 _____

Other Tasks

- ■ _____
- ■ _____
- ■ _____
- ■ _____
- ■ _____
- ■ _____
- ■ _____
- ■ _____
- ■ _____
- ■ _____

Who most needs your attention today?

Note To Self:

Train people well enough so they can leave, treat them well enough so they don't want to – Richard Branson

DAILY PLAN

M   T   W   T   F

DATE: /   /

My Big 3 For Today

1

2

3

Other Tasks

-
-
-
-
-
-
-
-
-
-

What do you need to communicate today?

Note To Self:

Great leaders communicate and great communicators lead
– Simon Sinek

WEEKLY REVIEW

DATE: /   /

My Biggest Wins

1
2
3
4
5

How Did I Get On With My Weekly Big 3?

1

2

3

Lessons Learnt This Week

1	
2	
3	
4	
5	

What Would I Do Differently If I Could Start This Week Again?

Determination and hard work are as important as talent. Yes, rejection and criticism hurt. Get used to it – Judy Blume

WEEKLY PLANNER

DATE: / /

My Big 3 For This Week

1
2
3

What Obstacles May Get In My Way And How I'll Overcome Them

Other Things To Do This Week

The Advice I Would Give Myself This Week Is

The end goal will feel meaningless if you've forgotten to enjoy the journey on the way – Charlotte Reed

DAILY PLAN

Ⓜ Ⓣ Ⓦ Ⓣ Ⓕ

DATE: / /

My Big 3 For Today
1
2
3

Other Tasks

- ▪
- ▪
- ▪
- ▪
- ▪
- ▪
- ▪
- ▪
- ▪
- ▪

What could you delegate today?

Note To Self:

Delegation requires the willingness to pay for short term failures in order to gain long term competency — Dave Ramsey

DAILY PLAN

M T W T F

DATE: / /

My Big 3 For Today

1
2
3

Other Tasks

- ■
- ■
- ■
- ■
- ■
- ■
- ■
- ■
- ■
- ■

What should you say no to today?

Note To Self:

Discipline is the bridge between goals and accomplishment
— Jim Rohn

DAILY PLAN

M   T   W   T   F

DATE: / /

My Big 3 For Today

1
2
3

Other Tasks

-
-
-
-
-
-
-
-
-
-

What meeting do you not need to be at today?

Note To Self:

The key is not to prioritise what's on your schedule but to schedule your priorities – Stephen Covey

DAILY PLAN

M   T   W   T   F

DATE: / /

My Big 3 For Today

1
2
3

Other Tasks

-
-
-
-
-
-
-
-
-
-

Who would benefit from your support today?

Note To Self:

When someone does something wrong, don't forget all the things they did right – Dr Travis Bradberry

DAILY PLAN

M   T   W   T   F

DATE: / /

My Big 3 For Today

1 _____

2 _____

3 _____

Other Tasks

- ☐ _____
- ☐ _____
- ☐ _____
- ☐ _____
- ☐ _____
- ☐ _____
- ☐ _____
- ☐ _____
- ☐ _____
- ☐

Is there a conversation you are putting off?

Note To Self:

A person's success in life can usually be measured by the number of uncomfortable conversations he or she is willing to have — Tim Ferris

WEEKLY REVIEW

DATE: / /

My Biggest Wins

1
2
3
4
5

How Did I Get On With My Weekly Big 3?

1
2
3

Lessons Learnt This Week

1
2
3
4
5

What Would I Do Differently If I Could Start This Week Again?

It's amazing what we can do if we simply refuse to give up
— Octavia Butler

MONTHLY REVIEW

Out of 5, how well did I progress on my 90 day goals?

Goal 1:

Goal 2:

Goal 3:

Goal 4:

How well did I lead my team this month?

I delegated well	1	2	3	4	5	N/A
I gave contructive feedback when needed	1	2	3	4	5	N/A
I made confident decisions	1	2	3	4	5	N/A
I kept my team motivated	1	2	3	4	5	N/A
I communicated goals and priorities successfully	1	2	3	4	5	N/A
I was good at managing my time and prioritising work	1	2	3	4	5	N/A
I asked for and acted on feedback	1	2	3	4	5	N/A
I managed upwards effectively	1	2	3	4	5	N/A
I coached my team rather than give them all the answers	1	2	3	4	5	N/A
I gave positive feedback when deserved	1	2	3	4	5	N/A
I felt confident in my ability as a manager	1	2	3	4	5	N/A

TAKING ACTION

The 3 Things I Notice About My Scores

What Actions Will I Take?

Find Management Top Tips at the end of the book
More free resources at www.thesmartermanager.com

WEEKLY PLANNER

DATE: / /

My Big 3 For This Week

1 _____

2 _____

3 _____

What Obstacles May Get In My Way And How I'll Overcome Them

_____

_____

_____

_____

_____

Other Things To Do This Week

_____   _____

_____   _____

_____   _____

_____   _____

_____   _____

_____   _____

The Advice I Would Give Myself This Week Is

_____

Whatever you can do, or dream you can do, begin it. Boldness has genius, power and magic in it. Begin it now — William H. Murray

DAILY PLAN

M   T   W   T   F

DATE: / /

My Big 3 For Today

1

2

3

Other Tasks

- [ ]
- [ ]
- [ ]
- [ ]
- [ ]
- [ ]
- [ ]
- [ ]
- [ ]
- [ ]

Is there someone you need to thank?

Note To Self:

A lot of people have gone further than they thought they could because someone else thought they could – Zig Ziglar

DAILY PLAN

M   T   W   T   F

DATE: /   /

My Big 3 For Today

1
2
3

Other Tasks

-
-
-
-
-
-
-
-
-
-

Who could you ask for help?

Note To Self:

Great things in business are never done by one person, they're done by a team of people – Steve Jobs

DAILY PLAN

M   T   W   T   F

DATE: / /

My Big 3 For Today

1
2
3

Other Tasks

-
-
-
-
-
-
-
-
-
-

How can you make today more fun?

Note To Self:

Be bold. Envision yourself living a life that you love
— Suzan-Lori Parks

DAILY PLAN

M   T   W   T   F

DATE: / /

My Big 3 For Today

1 _____

2 _____

3 _____

Other Tasks

- ▪ _____
- ▪ _____
- ▪ _____
- ▪ _____
- ▪ _____
- ▪ _____
- ▪ _____
- ▪ _____
- ▪ _____
- ▪ _____

What is your biggest opportunity today?

Note To Self:

Today is your opportunity to build the tomorrow you want
— Ken Poirot

DAILY PLAN

M   T   W   T   F

DATE: /   /

My Big 3 For Today

1 _____

2 _____

3 _____

Other Tasks

- _____
- _____
- _____
- _____
- _____
- _____
- _____
- _____
- _____
- _____

What assumptions are you taking into today?

Note To Self:

The only limit to our realization of tomorrow will be our doubts of today.
Let us move forward with strong and active faith – Franklin Roosevelt

WEEKLY REVIEW

DATE: /   /

My Biggest Wins

1
2
3
4
5

How Did I Get On With My Weekly Big 3?

1

2

3

Lessons Learnt This Week

1
2
3
4
5

What Would I Do Differently If I Could Start This Week Again?

Success is not final; failure is not fatal: it is the courage to continue that counts – Winston Churchill

WEEKLY PLANNER

DATE: / /

My Big 3 For This Week

1

2

3

What Obstacles May Get In My Way And How I'll Overcome Them

Other Things To Do This Week

The Advice I Would Give Myself This Week Is

When there's a hill to climb, don't think waiting will make it smaller
— Anon

DAILY PLAN

M   T   W   T   F

DATE: /   /

My Big 3 For Today

1 _____

2 _____

3 _____

Other Tasks

- ◼ _____
- ◼ _____
- ◼ _____
- ◼ _____
- ◼ _____
- ◼ _____
- ◼ _____
- ◼ _____
- ◼ _____
- ◼ _____

How can you be more creative today?

Note To Self:

The only courage you ever need is the courage to fulfil the dreams of your own life – Oprah Winfrey

DAILY PLAN

M   T   W   T   F

DATE: /   /

My Big 3 For Today

1 _____

2 _____

3 _____

Other Tasks

- ☐ _____
- ☐ _____
- ☐ _____
- ☐ _____
- ☐ _____
- ☐ _____
- ☐ _____
- ☐ _____
- ☐ _____
- ☐ _____

What are you tolerating?

Note To Self:

Do not let what you cannot do interfere with what you can do
— John Wooden

DAILY PLAN

(M) (T) (W) (T) (F)   DATE: / /

My Big 3 For Today

1 _____
2 _____
3 _____

Other Tasks

- ■ _____
- ■ _____
- ■ _____
- ■ _____
- ■ _____
- ■ _____
- ■ _____
- ■ _____
- ■ _____
- ■ _____

What do you need to leave alone today?

Note To Self:

Before you become a leader, success is all about growing yourself. After you become a leader, success is about growing others – Jack Welch

DAILY PLAN

M   T   W   T   F

DATE: /   /

My Big 3 For Today

1

2

3

Other Tasks

- ▪
- ▪
- ▪
- ▪
- ▪
- ▪
- ▪
- ▪
- ▪
- ▪

What will make you feel good today?

Note To Self:

I come in peace, but I mean business
— Janelle Monáe

DAILY PLAN

M T W T F

DATE: / /

My Big 3 For Today

1
2
3

Other Tasks

-
-
-
-
-
-
-
-
-
-

What question should you ask yourself?

Note To Self:

Quite often in life you have to ask yourself the question 'what am I waiting for?' – Charlotte Reed

WEEKLY REVIEW

DATE: / /

My Biggest Wins

1
2
3
4
5

How Did I Get On With My Weekly Big 3?

1
2
3

Lessons Learnt This Week

1
2
3
4
5

What Would I Do Differently If I Could Start This Week Again?

If you were ready for it, it wouldn't be growth
— James Clear

WEEKLY PLANNER

DATE: / /

My Big 3 For This Week

1 _____

2 _____

3 _____

What Obstacles May Get In My Way And How I'll Overcome Them

_____

_____

_____

_____

_____

Other Things To Do This Week

_____ _____

_____ _____

_____ _____

_____ _____

_____ _____

_____ _____

The Advice I Would Give Myself This Week Is

_____

I remind myself every morning: nothing I say this day will teach me anything. So, if I'm going to learn, I must do it by listening — Larry King

DAILY PLAN

M   T   W   T   F

DATE: /   /

My Big 3 For Today

1 _____

2 _____

3 _____

Other Tasks

- ☐ _____
- ☐ _____
- ☐ _____
- ☐ _____
- ☐ _____
- ☐ _____
- ☐ _____
- ☐ _____
- ☐ _____
- ☐ _____

What are you resisting?

Note To Self:

A good plan violently executed today is better than a perfect plan tomorrow – Gen George S. Patton

DAILY PLAN

M T W T F   DATE: / /

My Big 3 For Today

1

2

3

Other Tasks

-
-
-
-
-
-
-
-
-
-

Where are you too comfortable?

Note To Self:

If you limit your goals to what you know you can achieve, you're setting the bar way too low — Ray Dalio

DAILY PLAN

M   T   W   T   F

DATE: /   /

My Big 3 For Today

1 _____

2 _____

3 _____

Other Tasks

- _____
- _____
- _____
- _____
- _____
- _____
- _____
- _____
- _____
- _____

Where are you sabotaging yourself?

Note To Self:

We don't raise to the level of our goals; we sink to the level of our systems
— James Clear

DAILY PLAN

M   T   W   T   F

DATE: / /

My Big 3 For Today

1

2

3

Other Tasks

-
-
-
-
-
-
-
-
-
-

What will bring you joy today?

Note To Self:

It's not fun to fail, but it just might be the only way to succeed
— Jeff Goins

DAILY PLAN

M   T   W   T   F

DATE: / /

My Big 3 For Today

1 _____

2 _____

3 _____

Other Tasks

- ◼ _____
- ◼ _____
- ◼ _____
- ◼ _____
- ◼ _____
- ◼ _____
- ◼ _____
- ◼ _____
- ◼ _____
- ◼ _____

Where are you limiting yourself?

Note To Self:

Argue for your limitations and you get to keep them
— Unknown

WEEKLY REVIEW

DATE: /   /

My Biggest Wins

1
2
3
4
5

How Did I Get On With My Weekly Big 3?

1

2

3

Lessons Learnt This Week

1
2
3
4
5

What Would I Do Differently If I Could Start This Week Again?

Leadership is influence, we're leading all the time. We're influencing those around us in the right direction or the wrong direction – Kevin Kruse

WEEKLY PLANNER

DATE: / /

My Big 3 For This Week

1 _____
2 _____
3 _____

What Obstacles May Get In My Way And How I'll Overcome Them

_____
_____
_____
_____
_____

Other Things To Do This Week

_____   _____
_____   _____
_____   _____
_____   _____
_____   _____
_____   _____
_____   _____

The Advice I Would Give Myself This Week Is

_____

Amateurs sit and wait for inspiration, the rest of us just get up and go to work — Stephen King

DAILY PLAN

M   T   W   T   F   DATE: /   /

My Big 3 For Today

1 _____

2 _____

3 _____

Other Tasks

- _____
- _____
- _____
- _____
- _____
- _____
- _____
- _____
- _____
- _____

What are you pretending to know?

Note To Self:

You can never prove you are incapable of anything. You can only say you haven't achieved it yet – Joseph O'Connor

DAILY PLAN

M   T   W   T   F   DATE: / /

My Big 3 For Today

1 _____

2 _____

3 _____

Other Tasks

- _____
- _____
- _____
- _____
- _____
- _____
- _____
- _____
- _____
- _____

When are you unable to laugh at yourself?

Note To Self:

Self-confidence is the first requisite to great undertakings
– Samuel Johnson

DAILY PLAN

M   T   W   T   F   DATE: /   /

My Big 3 For Today

1 _____

2 _____

3 _____

Other Tasks

- _____
- _____
- _____
- _____
- _____
- _____
- _____
- _____
- _____
- _____

What feels overwhelming at the moment?

Note To Self:

Take care of the minutes and the hours will take care of themselves
– Lord Chesterfield

DAILY PLAN

M   T   W   T   F

DATE: /   /

My Big 3 For Today

1 _____

2 _____

3 _____

Other Tasks

- ■ _____
- ■ _____
- ■ _____
- ■ _____
- ■ _____
- ■ _____
- ■ _____
- ■ _____
- ■ _____
- ■ _____

Who are you most looking forward to talk to today?

Note To Self:

If everyone is moving forward together, then success takes care of itself
— Henry Ford

DAILY PLAN

M　T　W　T　F

DATE: / /

My Big 3 For Today

1 _____
2 _____
3 _____

Other Tasks

- ■ _____
- ■ _____
- ■ _____
- ■ _____
- ■ _____
- ■ _____
- ■ _____
- ■ _____
- ■ _____
- ■ _____

How could you guide someone today?

Note To Self:

Talent wins games, but teamwork and intelligence wins championships
— Michael Jordan

WEEKLY REVIEW

DATE: /   /

My Biggest Wins

1
2
3
4
5

How Did I Get On With My Weekly Big 3?

1

2

3

Lessons Learnt This Week

1
2
3
4
5

What Would I Do Differently If I Could Start This Week Again?

Become the kind of leader that people would follow voluntarily, even if you had no title or position – Brian Tracy

MONTHLY REVIEW

Out of 5, how well did I progress on my 90 day goals?

Goal 1:   Goal 2:   Goal 3:   Goal 4:

☐   ☐   ☐   ☐

How well did I lead my team this month?

I delegated well	1 2 3 4 5 N/A
I gave contructive feedback when needed	1 2 3 4 5 N/A
I made confident decisions	1 2 3 4 5 N/A
I kept my team motivated	1 2 3 4 5 N/A
I communicated goals and priorities successfully	1 2 3 4 5 N/A
I was good at managing my time and prioritising work	1 2 3 4 5 N/A
I asked for and acted on feedback	1 2 3 4 5 N/A
I managed upwards effectively	1 2 3 4 5 N/A
I coached my team rather than give them all the answers	1 2 3 4 5 N/A
I gave positive feedback when deserved	1 2 3 4 5 N/A
I felt confident in my ability as a manager	1 2 3 4 5 N/A

TAKING ACTION

The 3 Things I Notice About My Scores

What Actions Will I Take?

Find Management Top Tips at the end of the book
More free resources at www.thesmartermanager.com

WEEKLY PLANNER

DATE: / /

My Big 3 For This Week

1

2

3

What Obstacles May Get In My Way And How I'll Overcome Them

Other Things To Do This Week

The Advice I Would Give Myself This Week Is

The secret of getting ahead is getting started — Anon

DAILY PLAN

M   T   W   T   F

DATE: /   /

My Big 3 For Today

1 _____

2 _____

3 _____

Other Tasks

- _____
- _____
- _____
- _____
- _____
- _____
- _____
- _____
- _____
- _____

Who should you check in with today?

Note To Self:

Things work out best for those who make the best out of how things work out – John Wooden

DAILY PLAN

M T W T F

DATE: / /

My Big 3 For Today

1 _____

2 _____

3 _____

Other Tasks

- [ ] _____
- [ ] _____
- [ ] _____
- [ ] _____
- [ ] _____
- [ ] _____
- [ ] _____
- [ ] _____
- [ ] _____
- [ ] _____

What will make today a success?

Note To Self:

You may have the greatest bunch of individual stars in the world, but if they don't play together, the club won't be worth a dime — Babe Ruth

DAILY PLAN

M   T   W   T   F

DATE: / /

My Big 3 For Today

1

2

3

Other Tasks

-
-
-
-
-
-
-
-
-
-

What will make you smile today?

Note To Self:

Whoever you look up to, or put on a pedestal, know that they have fears too. They just learned how to push past it – Leila Ali

DAILY PLAN

M T W T F

DATE: / /

My Big 3 For Today

1 _____

2 _____

3 _____

Other Tasks

- ☐ _____
- ☐ _____
- ☐ _____
- ☐ _____
- ☐ _____
- ☐ _____
- ☐ _____
- ☐ _____
- ☐ _____
- ☐ _____

How can you help someone grow today?

Note To Self:

The time will never be 'just right'. Start where you stand, and work with whatever tools you may have at your command— Napoleon Hill

DAILY PLAN

M   T   W   T   F   DATE: /   /

My Big 3 For Today

1 _____

2 _____

3 _____

Other Tasks

- ☐ _____
- ☐ _____
- ☐ _____
- ☐ _____
- ☐ _____
- ☐ _____
- ☐ _____
- ☐ _____
- ☐ _____
- ☐

When are you too hard on yourself?

Note To Self:

Your calm mind is your ultimate weapon against your challenges –
Bryant McGill

WEEKLY REVIEW

DATE: / /

My Biggest Wins

1
2
3
4
5

How Did I Get On With My Weekly Big 3?

1

2

3

Lessons Learnt This Week

1
2
3
4
5

What Would I Do Differently If I Could Start This Week Again?

Hire people who are better than you are, then leave them to get on with it
— David Ogilvy

WEEKLY PLANNER

DATE: / /

My Big 3 For This Week

1 _____

2 _____

3 _____

What Obstacles May Get In My Way And How I'll Overcome Them

_____

_____

_____

_____

_____

Other Things To Do This Week

_____   _____

_____   _____

_____   _____

_____   _____

_____   _____

_____   _____

The Advice I Would Give Myself This Week Is

_____

Start before you are ready. Don't prepare, begin — Mel Robbins

DAILY PLAN

M T W T F

DATE: / /

My Big 3 For Today

1 _____

2 _____

3 _____

Other Tasks

- ☐ _____
- ☐ _____
- ☐ _____
- ☐ _____
- ☐ _____
- ☐ _____
- ☐ _____
- ☐ _____
- ☐ _____
- ☐ _____

How can you move out of your comfort zone today?

Note To Self:

Expect the best, plan for the worst, and prepare to be surprised.
— Denis Waitley

DAILY PLAN

M   T   W   T   F   DATE: /   /

My Big 3 For Today

1

2

3

Other Tasks

-
-
-
-
-
-
-
-
-
-

What possibilities are you not seeing?

Note To Self:

Delegating means letting others become experts and hence the best
— Timothy Firnstahl

DAILY PLAN

M   T   W   T   F

DATE: /   /

My Big 3 For Today

1 _____

2 _____

3 _____

Other Tasks

- _____
- _____
- _____
- _____
- _____
- _____
- _____
- _____
- _____
- _____

Who should you get to know better?

Note To Self:

It's teamwork that remains the ultimate competitive advantage, both because it is so powerful and so rare — Patrick Lencioni

DAILY PLAN

M   T   W   T   F

DATE: /   /

My Big 3 For Today

1 _____

2 _____

3 _____

Other Tasks

- _____
- _____
- _____
- _____
- _____
- _____
- _____
- _____
- _____
- _____

What is motivating you right now?

Note To Self:

Once you have commitment, you need the discipline and hard work to get you there – Haile Gebrselassie

DAILY PLAN

M   T   W   T   F

DATE: /   /

My Big 3 For Today

1 _____

2 _____

3 _____

Other Tasks

- ☐ _____
- ☐ _____
- ☐ _____
- ☐ _____
- ☐ _____
- ☐ _____
- ☐ _____
- ☐ _____
- ☐ _____
- ☐ _____

What do you you need to learn today?

Note To Self:

Courage is what it takes to stand up and speak; courage is also what it takes to sit down and listen. — Winston Churchill

WEEKLY REVIEW

DATE: / /

My Biggest Wins

1 _____
2 _____
3 _____
4 _____
5 _____

How Did I Get On With My Weekly Big 3?

1 _____
_____
2 _____
_____
3 _____
_____

Lessons Learnt This Week

1 _____
2 _____
3 _____
4 _____
5 _____

What Would I Do Differently If I Could Start This Week Again?

_____

Don't bother telling the world you are ready. Show it. Do it
— Peter Dinklage

WEEKLY PLANNER

DATE: / /

My Big 3 For This Week

1
2
3

What Obstacles May Get In My Way And How I'll Overcome Them

Other Things To Do This Week

The Advice I Would Give Myself This Week Is

Your future is created by what you do today, not tomorrow — Anon

DAILY PLAN

M T W T F

DATE: / /

My Big 3 For Today

1

2

3

Other Tasks

- ☐
- ☐
- ☐
- ☐
- ☐
- ☐
- ☐
- ☐
- ☐
- ☐

Who can you learn from today?

Note To Self:

The art of effective listening is essential to clear communication, and clear communication is necessary to management – James Cash Penney

DAILY PLAN

M   T   W   T   F

DATE: /   /

My Big 3 For Today

1 _____

2 _____

3 _____

Other Tasks

- ▪ _____
- ▪ _____
- ▪ _____
- ▪ _____
- ▪ _____
- ▪ _____
- ▪ _____
- ▪ _____
- ▪ _____
- ▪ _____

What feedback do you need to give today?

Note To Self:

Feedback is the breakfast of champions – Ken Blanchard

DAILY PLAN

M   T   W   T   F   DATE: /   /

My Big 3 For Today

1 _____

2 _____

3 _____

Other Tasks

- _____
- _____
- _____
- _____
- _____
- _____
- _____
- _____
- _____
- _____

What are you missing?

Note To Self:

Insight without action is worthless
— Phil Mcgraw

DAILY PLAN

M   T   W   T   F   DATE: /   /

My Big 3 For Today

1 _____

2 _____

3 _____

Other Tasks

- ☐ _____
- ☐ _____
- ☐ _____
- ☐ _____
- ☐ _____
- ☐ _____
- ☐ _____
- ☐ _____
- ☐ _____
- ☐ _____

What would make you feel stronger today?

Note To Self:

Having just one person who goes, 'Don't be stupid — of course you could handle that,' does actually rewire your brain — Caitlin Moran

DAILY PLAN

M   T   W   T   F

DATE: /   /

My Big 3 For Today

1 _____

2 _____

3 _____

Other Tasks

- ◼ _____
- ◼ _____
- ◼ _____
- ◼ _____
- ◼ _____
- ◼ _____
- ◼ _____
- ◼ _____
- ◼ _____
- ◼ _____

How could you make today easier?

Note To Self:

The key to teamwork is to learn a role, accept a role, and strive to become excellent playing it – Pat Riley

WEEKLY REVIEW

DATE: / /

My Biggest Wins

1 _____
2 _____
3 _____
4 _____
5 _____

How Did I Get On With My Weekly Big 3?

1 _____
_____

2 _____
_____

3 _____
_____

Lessons Learnt This Week

1 _____
2 _____
3 _____
4 _____
5 _____

What Would I Do Differently If I Could Start This Week Again?

_____

Don't count the days, make the days count – Muhammed Ali

WEEKLY PLANNER

DATE: / /

My Big 3 For This Week

1
2
3

What Obstacles May Get In My Way And How I'll Overcome Them

Other Things To Do This Week

The Advice I Would Give Myself This Week Is

Every day brings new choices — Martha Beck

DAILY PLAN

M   T   W   T   F   DATE: /   /

My Big 3 For Today

1 _____

2 _____

3 _____

Other Tasks

- ◼ _____
- ◼ _____
- ◼ _____
- ◼ _____
- ◼ _____
- ◼ _____
- ◼ _____
- ◼ _____
- ◼ _____
- ◼ _____

What do you need to let go of today?

Note To Self:

Sometimes letting go is an act of far greater power than hanging on
— Eckhart Tolle

DAILY PLAN

M   T   W   T   F

DATE: /   /

My Big 3 For Today

1
2
3

Other Tasks

-
-
-
-
-
-
-
-
-
-

What do you need to give your full attention to today?

Note To Self:

I learned that we can do anything, but we can't do everything, at least not at the same time. Timing is everything — Dan Millman

DAILY PLAN

M   T   W   T   F

DATE: /   /

My Big 3 For Today

1 _____

2 _____

3 _____

Other Tasks

- ☐ _____
- ☐ _____
- ☐ _____
- ☐ _____
- ☐ _____
- ☐ _____
- ☐ _____
- ☐ _____
- ☐ _____
- ☐ _____

What question should you ask today?

Note To Self:

A wise person can learn more from a foolish question than a fool can learn from a wise answer – Bruce Lee

DAILY PLAN

M   T   W   T   F

DATE: /   /

My Big 3 For Today

1

2

3

Other Tasks

- ▪
- ▪
- ▪
- ▪
- ▪
- ▪
- ▪
- ▪
- ▪
- ▪

How will you recharge your batteries today?

Note To Self:

Sometimes the most productive thing you can do is relax — Mark Black

DAILY PLAN

M   T   W   T   F

DATE: /   /

My Big 3 For Today

1 _____

2 _____

3 _____

Other Tasks

- ◼ _____
- ◼ _____
- ◼ _____
- ◼ _____
- ◼ _____
- ◼ _____
- ◼ _____
- ◼ _____
- ◼ _____
- ◼ _____

What expectations do you need to clarify?

Note To Self:

Communication leads to community, that is, to understanding, intimacy and mutual valuing – Rollo May

WEEKLY REVIEW

DATE: /   /

My Biggest Wins

1
2
3
4
5

How Did I Get On With My Weekly Big 3?

1

2

3

Lessons Learnt This Week

1
2
3
4
5

What Would I Do Differently If I Could Start This Week Again?

Life is not a problem to be solved, but a reality to be experienced
– Soren Kierkegaard

MONTHLY REVIEW

Out of 5, how well did I progress on my 90 day goals?

Goal 1: ☐   Goal 2: ☐   Goal 3: ☐   Goal 4: ☐

How well did I lead my team this month?

I delegated well	1	2	3	4	5	N/A
I gave contructive feedback when needed	1	2	3	4	5	N/A
I made confident decisions	1	2	3	4	5	N/A
I kept my team motivated	1	2	3	4	5	N/A
I communicated goals and priorities successfully	1	2	3	4	5	N/A
I was good at managing my time and prioritising work	1	2	3	4	5	N/A
I asked for and acted on feedback	1	2	3	4	5	N/A
I managed upwards effectively	1	2	3	4	5	N/A
I coached my team rather than give them all the answers	1	2	3	4	5	N/A
I gave positive feedback when deserved	1	2	3	4	5	N/A
I felt confident in my ability as a manager	1	2	3	4	5	N/A

TAKING ACTION

The 3 Things I Notice About My Scores

What Actions Will I Take?

Find Management Tips at the end of the book
More free resources at www.thesmartermanager.com

Management Tips

Valuable 1:1s

- What do you want to achieve with your 1:1s? Don't let them be just a box-ticking exercise.
- Come prepared and ask them to as well. You may get better discussion if you send some questions in advance for them to think about.
- Ask open, specific questions. Vague questions (ie How's things?) will get vague answers

Set clear expecations

- What assumptions are you making? What you think they know or understand may not be true
- Write down what you want them to know. Make your expectations very clear and leave no room for ambiguity
- Get them to summarise back what they understand they need to do to check for miscommunications or misunderstandings.

Have honest conversations

- ALWAYS listen first. Hear what they have to say before sharing your thoughts. You may learn something that will change your response
- Prepare the opening to the conversation. 'Can I give you some feedback' will often put people on the defensive. Invite the person into a two way conversation.
- We often avoid these because they makes us feel awkward. These conversations are not about us, they are about helping your team member grow in a supportive way.

Run useful Team meetings

- Every team is different. Work with your team to understand how they want to structure the team meetings. Discuss why you want to meet and desired outcomes
- Use them as an opportunity to get to know each other. Think about different ways to do this
- The best meetings are action based not just talking. What can you all prep before to make the most of the time you have together

Management Tips

Give regular feedback

- Give feedback (positive and constructive) as close to the moment as possible
- Be specific about what you are giving feedback on to give them clarity on what to continue - or stop - doing. 'Great job' is not specific enough
- Focus on behaviour (and desired action), not on their personality traits

Commincating goals

- Build that sense of 'being up to something together' by working with your team to build the goals.
- Relate any task you delegate back to the bigger goals. Give them the 'why'
- Don't be afraid to repeat the goals frequently. If you share them only once, it's unlikely they will be absorbed

Actively Listen

- You know this one, but do you do it?! Turn off all notifications during your conversations!
- Tune into their body language. Is it in agreement with the words they are saying
- When they are talking, think about what they are saying and not how you will respond. It's OK to pause a little to formulate your response once they have finished.

Know your team

- Be observant of the team dynamics. How do they get on? Any changes in how they are all working together? What strengths do they each bring?
- Understand a little about their world outside of work
- Prioritise being fair. Always.

Treat your team members like individuals

- Find out what they enjoy about their job and what they don't
- Recognise that everyone has different working styles
- Help them develop and utilise their strengths more

Management Tips

Seek to build trust

- Remember that small, consistent positive actions all contribute to an environment of trust ie giving them credit, not blaming, positive reinforcement, being their champion.
- Demonstrate early that you have their back
- Give them autonomy to get on with their work as soon as you can. Treat failure as a learning opportunity

Recognise challenges

- Be empathetic about obstacles in their way
- Empower them to move an obstacle that is in their control, help them when the control is with you, work together to succeed despite the obstacle if it is something that is unmoveable
- Take time with them to reflect on how things went once the challenge is overcome

Celebrate successes

- Celebrate effort and hard work as well as successes
- Think about what celebrations suit your team (not every one likes a social night out)
- You can still celebrate even if you are remote. Come up with creative ideas as a team

Have clarity on goals

- Be clear the short term goals of the team
- Be clear on longer term goals of the business
- Make sure your team have the same level of clarity. (If I asked them, could they tell me what the team goals are?)

Delegate effectively

- Be aware of the excuses you are making not to delegate - find a way around them
- Set really clear expectations when you delegate a task - don't assume they know
- Find a way to delegate once - video the handover session so they can rewatch it

Management Tips

Be clear on priorities

- Discuss your weekly priorities with your team (and check in with your manager)
- Refer back to them when a new issue arises that requires your team's time
- Be logical in your approach when prioritising work

Understand the roles of your team members

- If they are more of an expert than you, spend some time with them to understand the fundamentals
- Understand the challenges they face in their role and ask how you can best support them
- Find them a subject matter expert to be a mentor if appropriate. Remember your competence should be about great leadership and not necessarily technical expertise

Actively seek feedback and act on it

- Ask for specific feedback Instead of 'how am I doing?' ask 'in the last project, what's one way I could have supported you better?'
- Receive it graciously, ensuring that you fully understand it.
- Take action where appropriate and share your intentions with the feedback giver

Help your team develop

- Don't just focus on developing weaknesses - imagine the impact if they enhanced their strengths!
- Where are the skill gaps in your team - who would enjoy developing in that area?
- It doesn't have to be training - consider shadowing/being mentored/secondment/attending a conference/reading a book...

Understand the business

- Widen your scope of understanding by meeting with peers from different departments
- Research the industry
- Seek to regularly learn something new about the company or industry

Management Tips

Recognise strengths

- Ask them what a great day at work is for them - this may identify the strengths they have
- Ask if they have anything they are good at that they are not currently using at work - it may uncover some hidden treasures
- Find a way to use their strengths more - people are generally happier when they can

Coach your team members

- Be mindful of when you are jumping in with answers. Encourage your team members to at least think of a solution to a problem themselves - they often can.
- When they come and ask you for a solution ask them 'what do you think the options are?'
- Think about when you are involved in a decision that you could delegate to someone else (which will empower them and help them grow too)

Focus on continuous improvement

- Have regular retrospectives with your team - what is going well, what is not?
- Prioritise what you will work on to improve. Be realistic! And set some actions
- Regularly self-assess. How could you improve as a manager?

Voice concerns or say no when necessary

- Remember you are closer to the day to day than your manager. It is important that you share any concerns they may not have considered
- Think of another option if possible rather than just pushing back
- Disagree then commit. Speak up but know that your manager may still go a different direction. It's important to commit fully to the way forward even if you are not in full agreement There may be reasons behind it they cannot share.

More free management resources at
www.thesmartermanager.com

Printed in Great Britain
by Amazon